Extreme Sports

A CHAPTER BOOK

BY LOUISE A. GIKOW

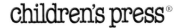

children's press®

A Division of Scholastic Inc.
New York Toronto London Auckland Sydney
Mexico City New Delhi Hong Kong
Danbury, Connecticut

For my daughter, Rachel—who is *extremely* terrific—
and knows when it's worth taking a risk!

ACKNOWLEDGMENTS

The author would like to thank all those who gave their time and
knowledge to help with this book: The International Surfing Museum in
Huntington Beach, California; Cris Whittaker; Tara Dakides; and Mat Hoffman.

Library of Congress Cataloging-in-Publication Data

Gikow, Louise.
  Extreme sports : a chapter book / by Louise A. Gikow.
    p. cm. – (True tales)
Includes bibliographical references and index.
  ISBN 0-516-23730-6 (lib. bdg.)   0-516-24683-6 (pbk.)
  1. Athletes–United States–Biography–Juvenile literature.
  2. Extreme sports–United States–Juvenile literature. I. Title. II. Series.

GV697.A1G49 2004
796.04 '6–dc22

                    2004000418

1 2 3 4 5 6 7 8 9 10 R 13 12 11 10 09 08 07 06 05 04

CONTENTS

INTRODUCTION

Extreme sports take people to the edge. They send people to the biggest waves. They carry people up the tallest mountains. They **propel** people off bridges and towers. They launch people high into the air.

In this book, you will be reading about people who have become **legendary** (LEJ-uhn-deh-ree) athletes in four different extreme sports. The sports are surfing, skateboarding, snowboarding, and **bicycle motocross** (BMX).

Duke Kahanamoku introduced surfing to the modern world. Tony Hawk is known as the greatest skateboarder of all time. Tara Dakides is on her way to snowboarding glory. Mat Hoffman is one of the best BMX riders.

People who do extreme sports make their own rules. They invent their own moves and often design their own courses or tracks. Even though they sometimes hurt themselves, their love for their sport always keeps them coming back for more.

CHAPTER ONE

HOPUPU FOR SURFING

It was a beautiful day on the island of O'ahu in Hawai'i. The skies were a rich blue. White clouds floated above Waikiki Beach. The waves lapped at the shoreline.

A small boy climbed into an **outrigger** canoe that sat on the sand. As he waited, two big men, his father and his uncle, pushed the canoe into the water. Then they jumped into the canoe and paddled out into the ocean.

When the two men had gotten far enough from shore, they stopped paddling.

Duke Kahanamoku

Duke Paoa Kahinu Mokoe Hulikohola Kahanamoku (that was the boy's name) was about to learn to swim. He would learn the way Hawaiians had always learned.

Duke's father picked him up. Then he tossed the boy over the side and into the water. Duke fell into the sea. Cool, salty water was all around him. As he sank beneath the waves, he started to paddle. He quickly bobbed to the surface.

His father and uncle smiled down at him. Duke would become a good "water man." In fact, Duke might become the greatest "water man" of all time.

Duke Kahanamoku was born on August 24, 1890, the oldest of six brothers. He was named after his father, who had been named after the Duke of Edinburgh. The English Duke visited Hawai'i in 1869. A number of Hawaiian boys of the time had been given the name "Duke" in honor of the visit.

Duke (far right) and his five brothers pose next to their surfboards.

The younger Duke was born in Honolulu but was brought up near the sea. He went to school across from Waikiki Beach. His family wanted him to enjoy the water. His mother let him swim out as far as he wanted. She didn't want him to be afraid of the water. He wasn't.

At fifteen, Duke became one of the original beach boys, surfing and swimming all the time. He was **hopupu** (HO-poo-poo) about surfing. *Hopupu* is a Hawaiian word that means *excited*.

This 1831 engraving shows Hawaiians surfing.

Polynesians (pol-uh-NEE-zhuns) have always been hopupu about surfing. They have been catching waves for thousands of years. They created **pictographs** of people surfing in 1500 B.C., more than 3,500 years ago. Surfing is one of the oldest sports in the world, and the oldest of all extreme sports.

The first surfers learned to body surf by holding their bodies stiffly. Then they let the waves carry them to shore. Next came body boards, surfboards that are known today as boogie boards. To ride them, people lay down flat. In order for people to stand upright on them, the boards had to become longer. Some boards were 18 feet (5 meters) long.

The current style of surfing comes from Hawai'i. Hawaiians call it *he'e nalu,* or wave sliding. Surfing almost disappeared from Hawai'i. In 1820, **missionaries** (MISH-uh-ner-eez) came to Hawai'i. The missionaries did not approve of the wild beach parties that went with surfing, so they preached against surfing. By 1890, when Duke was born, only a few surfers remained.

One of them was Princess Kailua. She was descended from Hawaiian royalty and was an expert surfer. She surfed Waikiki from about 1895 to 1899. Duke probably watched her surf when he was a boy.

In the early 1900s, big hotels began to be built on Waikiki Beach for **tourists** (TOOR-ists). Soon the tourists discovered the beach boys. They particularly noticed Duke, who was an impressive-looking young man.

An early photo of Duke

Duke with a longboard

He was more than 6 feet (1.8 meters) tall and had a swimmer's strong, slim body.

Duke soon found himself teaching tourists how to surf. To do so, he introduced the modern longboard. The longboard was big enough for two people. It let a student ride on the board with a teacher, which made surfing easier to learn.

In 1911, Duke entered a swimming **competition** (kom-puh-TISH-uhn) in Honolulu. He broke three world records there. A year later, he won a gold medal and a silver medal in the Stockholm Olympics. He also set a world record in the 100-meter **freestyle** swim.

Duke won another two gold medals for swimming in the 1920 Olympics in Antwerp, Belgium. He became known as the greatest swimmer in the world. He was finally defeated in 1924, when he was thirty-four years old. The man who beat him was only twenty years old. His name was Johnny Weissmuller. Later, Johnny became famous as the star of a number of "Tarzan" movies.

Duke acted in thirty movies himself. Although he never became as famous an actor as Johnny Weissmuller, he was famous around the world for surfing. When he

Duke gets ready to dive at a pre-Olympic swim meet.

talked about surfing, people listened. When he surfed, they watched. Duke introduced surfing to the East Coast of the United States. He brought surfing to Australia and helped make it popular in California.

A 2002 postage stamp of Duke

Surfing today is different from the way it was in the early days. Boards used to be made from heavy wood. Now they're made from lightweight **fiberglass**.

Lighter and better boards make it easier to do tricks. This is what makes surfing the extreme sport it is today. Doing tricks is called hotdogging.

Even if Duke didn't have a fiberglass board, he was still a pretty extreme surfer. In 1917, off Waikiki Beach, he rode a wave on his surfboard for more than a mile. That's extreme enough for any surfer, but it was all in a day's work for Duke.

A statue of Duke stands on Waikiki Beach.   15

CHAPTER TWO

THE GREATEST SKATEBOARDER

On June 27, 1999, thirty thousand people stood on Pier 30 in San Francisco. They were there for the fifth X Games. The crowd was waiting to see the Best Trick skateboarding competition. They were about to see skateboarding history.

Tony Hawk was competing that night. Tony, one of the greatest skateboarders, landed a great trick right away. It was a varial 720.

Tony Hawk

Fans watch Tony perform one of his tricks.

In this trick, Tony went up the ramp backward, spun twice, turned the skateboard around while in the air, and skated backward down the ramp.

Feeling good, he decided he'd try for a 900. The 900 is a very hard trick. Starting from the top of the ramp, you have to make two and a half turns in the air. Then you have to land and skate away clean.

Tony had been trying to do a 900 for more than ten years. A few years before, he had broken his rib trying. He had tried one for his video, *The End*, but failed. He had never landed a 900. No one had.

He didn't land his first try, so Tony tried again and again. In all, he tried the 900 eleven times that night. After a while, the other skateboarders stopped what they were doing to watch Tony.

At 8:32 P.M., Tony decided to try the 900 one more time. He flew up the U-shaped skating ramp, or **halfpipe**. He turned once.

He turned twice. He turned a half turn more. Then he came down. When his wheels slammed onto the ramp, he touched down lightly with his right hand. It took him a second before he realized what had happened. He had just landed a 900.

Tony received first prize that night. For Tony, it was a perfect moment. He said it was "the best moment of all time."

o gain speed, Tony skates from one edge of the halfpipe to the other. Then he takes off into the air.

In this move, Tony holds on to the bottom of the skateboard.

Tony has been skating since he was nine years old. That's when Steve, Tony's older brother, pulled out a dusty old blue skateboard from the garage. "Try this," Tony remembers Steve telling him.

In the beginning, Tony didn't love skateboarding. Then he visited Oasis Skatepark in San Diego, California. After that day was over, he was hooked. He wanted to try all the tricks he had seen. Tony kept riding at Oasis. He got better and started to enter competitions.

In 1982, when Tony was fourteen years old, he entered a skateboarding contest that paid prize money. Although Tony took third place, he didn't receive any money. Still, by entering the contest, Tony had become a **professional** skater. Two years later, he was the best in the world.

Tony has won twelve skateboarding world championships in his career. He has invented more than eighty tricks.

No one is sure how skateboarding got started. Some people think that surfers invented skateboarding in the early 1960s. Surfers wanted something to do when there were no waves. They pulled some wheels off their roller skates. They nailed them to some boards. Then they went "sidewalk surfing."

The surfers zoomed up and down the streets. They couldn't do much on their **makeshift** boards, though. Then rubber wheels were invented. Suddenly, the ride was smoother. The boards could move in different ways. The sidewalk surfers could do really cool moves.

In 1976, the first skateboard park was built. In the park skateboarders could zoom up ramps. After they reached the top and soared into the air, they could do turns. They could do flips and land backward.

Throughout Tony's career, the popularity of skateboarding has gone up and down. When Tony started, in the late seventies, it wasn't that popular. Then, in the late eighties, it caught on again. By the early nineties, many skateparks closed. Tony's career almost disappeared.

When the X Games started, skateboarding became popular again. It's so popular now that for the first time, there will be skateboarding in the 2004 Olympics.

Tony retired from skateboarding in 1999, so he won't be competing in the Olympics. You can be sure, though, that no matter what he's doing, he'll be watching.

Tony in action during the Tony Hawk Gigantic Skatepark Tour

CHAPTER THREE

SUPER COOL TARA

It was the fourth day of the 2001 X Games in Vermont. The air was crisp and cold on top of Mount Snow, but the heat was on Tara Dakides. Tara was the last snowboarder in the X Games 2001 Women's Big Air competition. If she could perform a perfect Rodeo 540, a backflip with one and a half spins, she would win. Could she do it?

Tara Dakides

Tara skates across an arch.

Each snowboarder had three chances to perform her most difficult trick. The judges had scored them based on the difficulty of the trick, how high they had gone, how far they had jumped, and how clean their landings were.

By the time it was Tara's turn, twenty-three women had already finished. Barrett Christy was in the lead. Tara was defending her gold in the 2000 X Games. She had already tried her trick twice, but she had missed both times.

Tara took a deep breath. She pushed off and flew down the hill. She lifted off into the air. When she landed clean, she knew she had done it. The judges agreed. They gave Tara a score of 89 and Barrett a score of 86.67. Tara had won again.

Girls have been snowboarding ever since the beginning of the sport. In fact, some people think the snowboard was invented for a girl.

In 1965 in Michigan, a dad named Sherman Poppen was watching his daughter ride her sled. Instead of lying down, she was standing on it.

Sherman tied two skis together to make it easier for her. Snowboarding was born.

In the 2002 Winter Olympics, an alpine rider zooms down a mountain.

There are different ways to snowboard. Some snowboarders like to zoom down hills. They're called Alpine riders. The word *alpine* comes from the word *Alps*. The Alps are a chain of tall mountains in Europe.

Other snowboarders like to do tricks. They do them in special snowboard parks. They use special snow tubes called halfpipes. These snowboarders are called freestylers. That's because their style of snowboarding is more free. It's also more extreme.

Snowboarding has become very popular. It is even an Olympic sport. In fact, it was the first extreme sport to be in the Olympic games. Although Olympic snowboarding first took place in 1998 in Japan, Tara didn't compete in the games. She didn't like the rules for the snowboarding competitions, so she stayed away.

Tara with her snowboard

Olympic snowboarders were only allowed two runs. This meant they had to be careful. They couldn't take a lot of risks. Taking risks is what snowboarding is about. After all, it's an extreme sport.

Tara takes risks. That's why she won a gold medal in the 2001 World Championships and five gold medals at the X Games. Tara competes in the halfpipe and **slopestyle** events as well as in Big Air. She's won medals in all of them. Tara has also won medals in bicycle stunt riding events. She's a skateboarder. She surfs. She skis. She writes poetry, too.

A few years ago, *Sports Illustrated* magazine named Tara one of the coolest women in sports. An interviewer asked Tara what being cool meant. Tara's definition was someone who could take a tumble and not be afraid of making "a complete idiot of herself." In other words, it was someone just like Tara Dakides.

Tara competing on a halfpipe made of snow

CHAPTER FOUR

WHO'S AFRAID OF A BIG, BAD BIKE?

Five days before Mat Hoffman was supposed to go to Brazil to do some stunt riding in bicycle shows, he broke his wrist. Most bikers would have cancelled the South America trip, but most bikers aren't Mat Hoffman.

Mat didn't want to let his fans down. So, early in 2002, he flew to Brazil. He took the cast off his arm and taped it so he could get a better grip on his bike.

First, Mat had to get used to a whole new ramp. He practiced some tricks and crashed a couple

Mat Hoffman

Mat performs before a huge crowd.

of times, but he didn't give up. He finally landed the trick he was going for.

Then he noticed three fans in the crowd. On their chests were the numbers 9-0-0. The numbers stand for the 900, a very difficult trick Mat had invented. When you do a 900, you do two and a half turns in the air.

Mat usually does what he feels like doing, but he couldn't let his fans down. He had to try a 900, even though he hadn't done one for more than seven years. Could he do it? Mat Hoffman performed it perfectly, broken wrist and all.

Mat has always loved being airborne. He loved it as a boy when he learned to jump on the family trampoline with his brothers, Travis and Todd. When Mat was nine years old, he got his first motorcycle, a Kawasaki KDX 80. Mat's cousin, Tom, helped teach him the ropes. Tom used to take Mat on motorcycle trips in the country around Edmond, Oklahoma. Tom also taught Mat about motocross, which is motorcycle racing.

Mat did some motorcycle racing himself. After a few bad **injuries** (IN-juh-reez), his parents took away the motorcycle and got

Mat a regular bike, a red Mongoose.

Extreme bike riding, known as bicycle motocross or BMX, started back in the 1960s. That's when a movie called *On Any Sunday* was shown in theaters. In the movie, a motorcycle racer named Mert Lawill zoomed around, doing tricks. He flew into the air. He twisted and turned.

Bike riders wanted to do the same things. They rode normal bikes, like 20-inch (51-centimeter) Schwinn Stingrays, but they didn't want to ride normally.

They started by doing jumps on dirt tracks. Then they noticed the skateboarders. They saw how the skateboarders flew up in the air. They wanted to be up in the air, too, so they built halfpipes and started doing tricks.

They jumped their bikes above the **coping**, the outer edge of the halfpipe. They turned in the air on their bikes. They flipped. They flew.

Today, there are two kinds of BMX riding. One is racing. The other is doing tricks on ramps. This is called freestyle or bicycle stunt. Mat does a special kind of bicycle stunt called **vert** riding. He uses a

Mat flies off a vert ramp into the air.

Mat at the X Games in San Francisco, California

vert ramp, which is sometimes called a halfpipe because it looks like a pipe that has been cut in half.

Mat is probably the greatest BMX vert rider. The first time Mat looked over the top of the ramp, he was very scared. Mat's brother Todd was holding him and his bike. Mat told Todd not to let go. Todd did.

After that first drop, Mat wanted to try it again and again. After he got the hang of it, he tried some tricks he had seen in BMX magazines. Then he invented his own tricks. If he knew a trick, he'd try to make it harder. He'd add another twist or turn. He'd go backward.

Mat started competing in freestyle BMX when he was fourteen years old. A year later he began touring with the Skyways team.

In January 1989, Mat went to a King of Vert event in Irvine, California. He won the

amateur (AM-uh-chur) competition. Then he turned professional, entered the pro competition, and won that, too. He also won the highest air contest.

A condor

Over the years, Mat invented many tricks that riders are still doing today. Mat invented the flair, a backward flip with a 180-degree twist. He invented the no-handed 540. He was the first person to successfully complete the 900. Without Mat, BMX would not be the same.

Mat's nickname is The Condor. A condor is a very large bird that flies high in the sky. The nickname makes sense. Like the bird he's named after, Mat spends a lot of time in the air.

He once went to Norway to go base-jumping. After a few jumps off a 3,200-foot (975-meter) cliff, Mat decided to do something different. He jumped off the cliff on his bike. What's more, he did a double backflip on his way down. Like all base jumpers, he had a parachute. Even so, it was extreme!

At the end of the 1980s, BMX freestyle was becoming less popular. Many bike companies were failing. So in 1991, Mat created his own company to support BMX freestyle. He got some great riders together. Then they toured the country to **promote** the sport.

During the tour, the bikes kept breaking. Mat and his team realized that the bikes weren't strong enough. Mat designed new BMX bicycles and sold them.

Mat has invented more than 120 tricks.

In 1992, Mat built a 21-foot (6-meter) vert **quarterpipe** (KWOR-tur-pipe). Then he jumped 23 feet (7 meters) into the air. This set the first high-air record.

Mat wanted to jump higher than that. In 2001, he jumped another, bigger vert quarterpipe. This time, he jumped 26.5 feet (8 meters) above the ramp. That put him more than 50 feet (15 meters) off the ground. No bike rider has ever jumped that high.

That day, Mat received a serious head injury. Besides being in a lot of pain, Mat suffered memory loss. At the time of the crash, Mat had a four-month-old baby girl named Gianna. Mat decided that he had to stop pushing so hard to go higher. He wanted to be around for his daughter.

Today Mat believes that "you can do anything you want as long as you are willing and able to face whatever challenge is presented to you."

43

GLOSSARY

amateur (AM-uh-chur) playing a sport for pleasure and not earning money from it

bicycle motocross (BMX) a form of extreme bicycle riding inspired by motocross (doing tricks on motorcycles) and skateboarding

competition (kom-puh-TISH-uhn) a contest

coping the lip along the top of a ramp or pipe used for skateboarding or BMX riding

extreme sport any sport that is considered dangerous and has high risk involved

fiberglass a lightweight material made of glass and plastic

freestyle a competition in which a contestant performs using any style he or she wants

halfpipe a ramp shaped like the letter U. Its sides are at a ninety-degree angle.

hopupu (HO-poo-poo) a Hawaiian word meaning *excited*

injury (IN-juh-ree) damage or harm done to someone

legendary (LEJ-uhn-deh-ree) having to do with legends, stories from long ago about amazing people

makeshift a word that describes something made out of whatever is handy

missionary (MISH-uh-ner-ee) someone who is sent to another country to teach the people there about his or her religion

outrigger a beam that is attached to a canoe to prevent it from tipping over

pictograph a picture carved on stone

Polynesians (pol-uh-NEE-zhunz) people who come from Polynesia, a group of islands in the Pacific Ocean

professional earning money from playing sports

promote to make other people aware of someone or something

propel to push something or someone forward

quarterpipe (KWOR-tur-pipe) a halfpipe with only one wall

slopestyle a snowboarding event in which snowboarders ride over different kinds of jumps

tourist (TOOR-ist) someone who travels to other places for enjoyment

vert short for *vertical*; a type of freestyle competition in which riders go straight up into the air

FIND OUT MORE

Hopupu for Surfing
www.hawaiianswimboat.com/duke.html
Read Duke's bio.

The Greatest Skateboarder
http://www.tonyhawk.com
Tony answers fans' questions on his official website.

Super Cool Tara
http://expn.go.com/athletes/bios/DAKIDES_TARA.html
Watch videos of Tara on the slopes.

Who's Afraid of a Big, Bad Bike?
www.ababmx.com
This site gives information on BMX rules and race results.

More Books to Read

BMX Bikes by Kathleen W. Deady and Terri Sievert, Capstone Press, 2001

Extreme Snowboarding by Pat Ryan, Capstone Press, 1998

Extreme Sports by Richard Platt, Dorling Kindersley Publishing, 2001

On the Halfpipe with Tony Hawk by Matt Christopher and Glenn Stout, Little, Brown, 2001

INDEX

PHOTO CREDITS

47

MEET THE AUTHOR

Louise A. Gikow has written hundreds of books, scripts, and songs for kids of all ages (and a few for adults, too). She lives in New York City with her husband, daughter, and two cats. She's worked for Jim Henson Productions and Nickelodeon, which was pretty exciting, but she has never done an extreme sport of any kind. Her cats, on the other hand, do jump off high bookcases without parachutes.

Louise thinks that people who do extreme sports are extremely brave, but suggests that kids remember that the athletes featured in this book are trained professionals. Children should not try any extreme sport without first asking an adult's permission.